101 Uses
for a
Yorkshireman's Wallet

written by
Ian McMillan
illustrated by
Tony Husband

Dalesman

First published in 2015 by Dalesman
an imprint of
Country Publications Ltd
The Water Mill, Broughton Hall
Skipton, North Yorkshire BD23 3AG
www.dalesman.co.uk

ISBN 978-1-85568-343-3

Typeset in Stone Informal.

Printed in China by 1010 Printing International Ltd.

Introduction

by Ian McMillan

When Tony Husband and I first thought about doing this book we wanted it to dispel some myths; he's from Lancashire and I'm a proud Yorkshireman and we thought that this book could examine the truth behind the long-standing idea that people from Yorkshire are tight, or stingy, or careful with money, or miserly, or quid-shy. I made that last one up, but it seems to express what I mean.

The initial idea was that Tony would draw cartoons showing the aforementioned tightness and stinginess, and I would delve into the vast and multifaceted archives of Yorkshire literature and folklore and come up with counterintuitive examples that showed the Yorkshire generosity of spirit.

We agreed to meet in a café on the Yorkshire/ Lancashire border to discuss the kind of material we would need to create. I offered to pay, again underlining the absolute fib of the tarnished idea of the quid-shy tyke. We had lovely cups of tea and cake, and then, when it came to pay the bill, I found that my wallet wouldn't open. It just wouldn't.

Try as I might, I couldn't get the thing to admit my fingers to get the money out. Tony, because he's a cartoonist, thought I was joking, but to his consternation found that he couldn't open it either; nor could anyone in the café, including a rugby team and an off-duty wallet opener from Slough.

Tony had to pay; I offered to give him my share of the money next time I saw him but, funnily enough, we've not bumped into each other since then. Maybe this was an omen, but in all my trawling through hundreds of years of Yorkshire history, I found no evidence of any denizens of the White Rose county being generous. So what follows is a true account, I'm sorry to say, of the Yorkshireman's relationship with money.

Hang on, that's Tony coming up our path for his money. I'll just hide behind the settee and he'll think I'm not in.

WELCOME

Walter Wall's Wallet Wall

Walter Wall, owner of the antiques emporium on Market Street, had a unique display in the back of the shop, the Wallet Wall. Over the years, in the pockets of old coats and in boxes packed away in attics that he'd bought in house clearances, he found many examples of the Yorkshireman's Wallet, including the Patent Weldshut, the NivverOppen, the Safe Deposit and The Trap. The first three were fairly common in the 1950s and 1960s but The Trap is a rarity of which only a limited number were produced before it was withdrawn due to finger and thumb loss.

It worked on the common-sense principle that even when a Yorkshireman opened his wallet he didn't really want to open his wallet, so the zip was fitted with a spring that would snap shut as the Yorkshireman attempted to open it, thus giving his fingers a bit of a bruising and reminding him that he didn't want to open it in the first place. The spring was too strong and the wallet was withdrawn from sale before any modification could be made.

Walter Wall's Wallet Wall can still be seen by special appointment on Tuesdays and Thursdays.

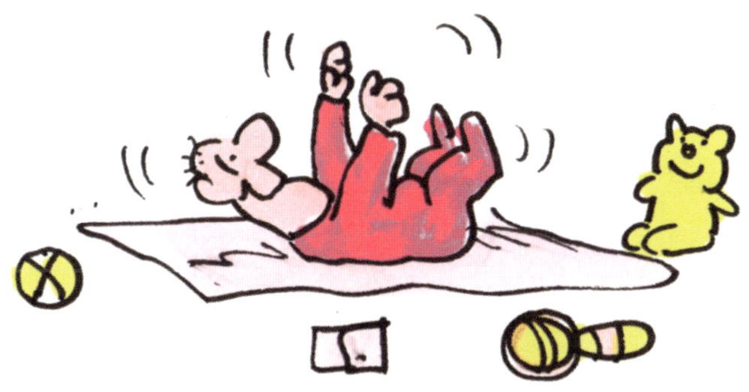

Yorkshire Wallet Moths

All these are examples of the Yorkshire Wallet Moth as collected over the years and displayed in the Natural History Museum in Wyke.

The Blind Leyburn Wallet Moth: This moth breeds in only the least-opened of Yorkshiremen's wallets, and so has been known to live in the dark for decades at a time. When the wallet is finally opened the moth will not come out unless a hood is placed over its head. It is not fully understood what it breeds with and how, without disturbing the second-class stamps.

The Ten Bob Note Eating Moth: This moth forages for food inside a Yorkshireman's wallet and has been known to eat not only ten bob notes but coins and driving licences.

The Wallet Myth Moth: A moth introduced to his wallet by naturalist John Huddersby to prove his thesis that Yorkshiremen were not stingy but were, in fact, generous. The moth refused to leave the wallet for many decades, even though John opened his wallet four times over that period, thus proving or disproving Huddersby's idea, depending on who you believe.

The Gomersal Coin Protector Moth: This moth has been bred over hundreds of years in back-alley moth-breeding farms to attack anyone who opens the wallet, whether or not the person opening the wallet is the owner of the wallet. If the Gomersal Coin Protector Moth finds its way into your wallet, you'll never be able to open your wallet again, which is fine by us.

The Mothosaurus: This is a prehistoric moth first found in the deer-hide wallets of early Yorkshiremen around the Plasticine period. Because it likes dark and cosy spaces, it has thrived in the wallets of Yorkshiremen through the ages and is on record as being the oldest continually breeding moth in history, now that the Lancashire Barm Pot Moth has died out.

The Math Moth: A moth introduced to Yorkshire from America, which, as well as living in your wallet, can add up all the loose change in the coin bit.

POETRY

Smollett's Wallet Limericks

A feller from Bradford called Smollett
Kept chickens and geese in his wallet
He said 'Get one of these.
Poultry-keeping's a breeze
Oh the beauty of this, I'll extol it:

'They live there in perfect conditions
Though the coinage can lead to restrictions
The smell and the dark
They think's quite a lark
and they nest in the notes (with permission).

'Yes, a wallet's a place for your birds
To deny that would just be absurd
They are not cramped.
It is not dark and damp.
Don't believe all the stuff that you've heard!

'Well, I'll leave you to make up your mind:
Is wallet bird-keeping unkind?
They're really well fed
With cash for a bed,
As a breeder I'm perfectly kind…'

What's your view on this? Join the online debate at www.walletchickens.co.uk

BOATING LAKE
7

'I can find my way into your heart but I can't find my way into your wallet'

A music-hall song, sung by Jessie Klondyke
the Scarborough Warbler

I can find my way straight into your heart
But your wallet is closed to me;
When you took me out for an apple tart
And a lovely cup of hot sweet tea
I said 'I've left me money in my hovel
And you, my love, will have to pay the bill.'
He started to weep and wail and grovel
Until I thought he'd have to take a pill;
I said 'Your wallet's there, get your money out, mate!'
He said 'I can't: I can't manipulate the zip!'
Well I tell you that did nothing for my heart rate
And then the waiter came and smacked him on the lip!
A Yorkshirman's wallet is his castle
And you can't get across the moat
To open up the wallet is a hassle
And it's murder trying to pull it from his coat!

CLIMBING WALL

The Rare Yorkshireman's Wallet Crocus

Botanists are excited by the discovery, in reclaimed land at the back of the former Gasworks in Pateley Bridge, of the very rare crocus known colloquially as the 'Yorkshireman's Wallet' because it never opens to reveal its flower, even in the brightest sunshine.

Dr Amy Tring, from the University of Mexborough, wrote in the *Yorkshire Journal of Rare Plants:* 'Scientists have for years wondered why this particular breed of crocus refuses to open, especially when a close relative of the plant which mainly flourishes in the south of England opens at any and every opportunity. Could it be the harsh Yorkshire climate? Could it be something in the soil? Or could it simply be that, like the Yorkshireman's Wallet, the flower refuses to give up its secrets?'

One Day in the Life of a Yorkshireman

Midnight: Switch light on. Check that wallet is still on bedside cupboard. Check that it looks full.

02.00: Switch light on. Tell wife to go back to sleep. Reach over to touch wallet. Feel reassured.

04.00: Switch light on. Reach over and pick wallet up. Wander around the bedroom with it in your hand, feeling its weight. Tell wife to go back to sleep.

06.00: Finally succumb and get up. Sit in kitchen making a cup of tea, gazing lovingly at the wallet.

08.00: Decide to take wallet for a walk. Put it in your jacket and feel the pleasant sensation of the wallet weighing the jacket down and making you lean to one side.

10.00: On the clifftop path, gaze at the sky and take your wallet out to show it the sun. Feel the pleasing weight of the wallet in your hand.

Midday: Call in station café for sandwich. Take wallet out to pay but then can't bear to open it so offer to pay next time you're in. The owner, a fellow Yorkshireman, understands.

14.00: Back in the house,

trying to arrange the wallet next to the window so that the afternoon light falls on it in a pleasing way.

16.00: Read a book with the wallet beside you on the settee like a faithful dog.

18.00: Cook the tea and insist on setting an extra place for the wallet, much to your wife's disgust.

20.00: Watch TV, the wallet nestling between you and your wife like a leather dog.

22.00: Bath. The wallet watches you from the sink.

Midnight: Bedtime. Wait until your wife is looking the other way then kiss the wallet goodnight.

Ode to the Yorkshireman's Wallet

by Obadiah Clemmit, bard, 1846-1893

O the Yorkshireman's wallet is a wondrous thing
With coins of many denominations it does ring
Pennies and florins of that I have no doubt
But you will never know how many because he won't ever open it to get the beggars out!

O the Yorkshireman's wallet is safe and secure
With more locks upon it than a prison cell door
The interior of the wallet has never seen the light
And in its depths it is darker than a deep coal mine in the middle of the darkest night!

O the Yorkshireman's wallet is an impenetrable temple
It's a thing of great complexity it cannot be described as simple
I myself have never seen a Yorkshireman put his hand inside one
I suppose that's in case he finds that the money he put inside it many years ago has actually gone!

O the Yorkshireman's wallet cannot ever be
breached
You may as well try to count all the grains of
sand on the beach
It will hold its secrets until the Yorkshireman's
dying day
And then we'll blow it up and spend all his
money in a pleasurable and exciting way!

Yorkshireman's Wallet Acrostic Poem

by Simon Linton, aged 9

Yorkshireman's wallet
Oh you are hard to get into;
Right difficult I'd say.
Kellie tried and she couldn't.
Steven tried and he couldn't.
Harry tried and he couldn't.
Iqbal tried and he couldn't.
Rose tried and she couldn't.
Edwina tried and she couldn't.
Mark tried and he couldn't.
Andrew tried and he couldn't.
Naomi tried and she couldn't.
Satnam tried and he couldn't.
William tried and he couldn't.
Alison tried and she couldn't.
Laura tried and she couldn't.
Lara tried and she couldn't.
Ekene tried and she couldn't.
Terri tried and she couldn't.

2/10 SEE ME!

YORKSHIRE
SCULPTURE
PARK

TONIGHT!

FOR ONE NIGHT ONLY

THE CELEBRATED

ESCAPOLOGIST

HARRY HOUDINI

will be ENTOMBED in that most HIGH SECURITY of all PRISONS

THE

YORKSHIREMAN'S WALLET

HE WILL THEN, IN A SPACE OF NOT MORE THAN FIFTEEN MINUTES, EFFECT AN ESCAPE FROM THIS LEATHERY COFFIN WHERE HE WILL BE ATTACKED BY ENORMOUS HUNGRY MOTHS!

THIS SPECTACLE MUST BE SEEN TO BE BELIEVED!

TICKETS ONE SHILLING

HOW MUCH?

One shilling.

Billy Burton's Letter to his Dear Old Mam

Bridlington 21st June 1927

Dear Mam,

Hope this finds you as it leaves us, what I mean is hope this finds you better than it leaves us because since this afternoon we, that is Dotty my wife and I, have been trapped indeed held against our will at the Ocean's Harvest Fish and Chip Shop in Bridlington.

After the wedding night and the nice breakfast at the Bide-A-Wee Guest House Dotty my wife and I went for a stroll on the beach and then to the Ocean's Harvest for fish and chips.

Imagine my surprise when at the end of our repast I found that the wallet you and Dad had bought me as a surprise wedding present would not open. I tried and Dotty (you know what big hands she has) tried and we could not open it. The owner of the chip shop and his son, a rugby player, tried and could not open it. A circus strongman and his family who were also buying fish and chips for the entire circus could not open it. The chip shop owner tried to peel the wallet open using an industrial-strength potato peeler but he couldn't.

I did not know what to do. I still do not know what to do. The police have arrived and their dog is worrying the wallet but it still refuses to open. They say that unless the wallet is opened and I can pay for the fish and chips my new wife Dotty and I will have to go to prison.

Could you come to Bridlington and pay the money soonest?

I know you live in Canada now but could you come to Bridlington and pay the money soonest?

Your loving son,

Billy (and Dotty)

The Yorkshireman's Wallet in Nature

A number of plants and animals are named after the Yorkshireman's Wallet. Here's a sample:

The Yorkshireman's Wallet Fly Trap Plant: all flies are safe around this plant because it never opens.

The Yorkshireman's Wallet Moth: flies in a very ungainly way because it cannot open its wings.

The Yorkshireman's Wallet Dolphin: the reputedly beautiful song of this aquatic mammal has never been heard because it won't open its mouth.

The Yorkshireman's Wallet Mistletoe: unsuccessful at Christmas because as soon as anyone comes close to it displaying symptoms of intimacy, it closes up even tighter than it was before so that you can't see the mistletoe berries.

The Yorkshireman's Wallet Lizard: its jaws can snap shut so tightly they can break thick and gnarled tree trunks.

YORKSHIRE FLOWER SHOW
A YORKSHIRE FLY TRAP

The Yorkshire Drag

scene 3 take 12 .. Action!

Pitch for Reality TV Series: The Yorkshireman's Wallet

In this ten-part series a number of Yorkshiremen will be given a wallet and the means to open it; inside the wallet they will find either a cheque for a hundred thousand pounds or A Cup of Hot Nowt.

Each Yorkshireman's endurance will be tested to the limit as, without any food or water, they have to stare at the wallet without opening it. One by one the Yorkshiremen will succumb to the temptation of opening to see if the hundred thousand pounds is inside.

The winner of the series will be the one who lasts longest.

Reality TV series cancelled after three shows

The Reality TV series The Yorkshireman's Wallet has been cancelled because, according to the producers, none of the Yorkshiremen involved showed any interest at all in opening the wallet, even with the promise of one of them having a fortune of a hundred thousand pounds inside. One of the Yorkshiremen explained: "Ah've nivver oppened a wallet yet and Ah dooant intend to start nah, even for a hundred thou, wallets are not built for oppenin!"

How Tight was Uncle Bernard?

Old Music Hall Song

How tight was Uncle Bernard?
How tight was Uncle Bern?
He was as tight as a Yorkshireman's wallet
As you're about to learn:

He always bought one trouser leg
He always bought one shoe
He hung one sleeve upon his peg
He bought one glove not two
He wore the same hat every day
For thirty years or more
He sent his children out to play
With an egg and a broken door
He never spent a penny piece
Let alone a quid
And his miserly ways they only ceased
When they nailed down the coffin lid!

CHORUS

TRYING TO GET FRANK OUT OF THE POND BY THROWING HIM YOUR HUGE WALLET TO FLOAT BACK TO SHORE ON

Frank. Don't panic. Here, look, I'm going to chuck you my wallet, the big one that I got from Whitby, and you can grab on to it and use it like a floatation device.

Ready, Frank? Right. Here goes! Don't forget. Hang on to it, hang on to it, kid. Hold on to it.

Ah.

It sunk. Just got paid, you see. All them ten-bob bits.

Sorry, Frank. You'll have to paddle.

SAFETY TIP IF YOU ARE CAUGHT OUT ON A MOUNTAIN IN A HIGH WIND (FROM T' TYKE'S BOOK O' SAFETY, *1898)*

If thou art on a mountain in t' dales o' Yorksheer and suddenly t' wind gets up an' blaws an' blaws and tha'r in danger o' being blooan all t' way ter Lankasheer, all tha has to do is get thi wallet art on thi pocket and hold it in thi 'and and tha'll not get blawn nowhere.

Tha might ask why tha can't just keep a stooan in thi pocket cos surely tha still wun't get blawn nowhere.

Aye! But t' fooerce o' t' wind might mek thi wallet rip thi kex and then tha'll hev to open thi wallet an' buy some new uns an' that'd nivver do!

The Glorious 12th Wallet shoot

Bill Tremayne and the Yorkshireman's Wallet Wrestling Hold

In the heyday of British wrestling in the mid-1960s one grappler from Featherstone was feared in every ring the length and breadth of the country. His name was Bill Tremayne and beneath this gentle-looking man's unassuming exterior beat the heart of a lion and, more importantly, the legs of a gorilla. Not literally of course: legs can't beat.

Tremayne had the strongest thighs in the business and he would simply lock them round an opponent's neck until the opponent went blue, purple, or an odd transparent colour. In a newspaper report of his epic battle against Admiral Blossom of Louth, 'the man with the full-sail biceps', his signature move was described as 'The Yorkshireman's Wallet', so hard were his legs to prise open, and the name stuck.

In later life, after retiring from the Grunt 'n' Groan industry, Tremayne became a popular attraction at local charity functions, challenging whole teams of people to attempt to separate his legs. None of them ever could and this particular Yorkshireman's Wallet remained unopened.

It was his last wish–
his ashes to be put in his
wallet and buried

References to A Yorkshireman's Wallet in Classic and Popular Literature

'He found the shellfish on the beach of the deserted island harder to open than A Yorkshireman's Wallet.'

Robinson Crusoe *by Daniel Defoe, p435.*

'Please sir, can I have some more? You've got more chance of getting into A Yorkshireman's Wallet, Oliver Twist!'

Oliver Twist *by Charles Dickens, p92.*

'I wandered lonely as the inside of A Yorkshireman's Wallet.'

First draft of Daffodils *by William Wordsworth.*

'Suddenly the great white whale appeared, as huge and solid and impenetrable as A Yorkshireman's Wallet.'

Moby Dick *by Herman Melville, p143.*

‘The name’s Bond, James Bond, said 007, his mouth barely open, like the entrance to A Yorkshireman’s Wallet.’

Dr No *by Ian Fleming, p209.*

‘He could not prife the money from hif grippe; Twaf held af though in A Yorkfhireman’f Wallet.’

The Moneylender’s Tale
by Geoffrey Chaucer.

THE BIG UN

Yorkshireman's Wallet manufacturers Beeston and Sons, of Halifax, hit the front pages of the national newspapers in 1972 when they created a wallet that was so large and so valuable that it had to be driven around on the back of a flat-bed truck and guarded by security men.

'The Big Un', as it was known, was thirteen yards long, eight yards wide and weighed almost a quarter of a ton. It was capable of holding not only the lifetime savings of any Yorkshireman or woman, but there were also bedrooms and a bathroom secured within its flaps and pockets, as well as a full-size snooker table and an indoor swimming pool.

The Big Un was launched at a special event at the Shay Stadium in Halifax in the high summer of 1972 with the slogan 'If tha wants a wallet, get a Big Un!'. Brass bands played, cheerleaders danced and free Yorkshire puddings were given out.

Sadly, the boss of Beeston's, passing the wallet-laden truck under the influence of too many Yorkshire puddings, suffered a foot injury when the wallet slipped and fell on him.

He didn't mind the injury so much, but he had to go to a rest home in Lancashire!

The Famous Yorkshireman's Wallet Sociological Experiment of 1959

In order to test the theory that Yorkshire people are grasping and tight, the Sociology Department at Leeds University carried out a study that has become a shining example of Yorkshire-based fieldwork in the years since it was first attempted in November 1959.

The experiment itself was simple: a ten pound note was placed on a busy street next to an apparently abandoned wallet; researchers hid in the upstairs room of a nearby butcher's shop and observed the proceedings. They created five classifications of Yorkshireness that could be applied to the passers-by who interacted, which have remained classics of their kind:

Ignores wallet and ten pound note — *not a Yorkshireman.*

Picks up wallet and ignores ten pound note — *Yorkshireman in need of a visit to the opticians.*

Picks up ten pound note and ignores wallet — *suspicious Yorkshireman who thinks he is having a trick played on him. Picks up ten pound note and tries to prise open the wallet to put it in, using The Time Honoured Methods.*

Picks up wallet and ten pound note and attempts to eat them — *Scotsman.*

Look, it's Wallet man!

BARNSLEY
ZOO

A Yorkshireman's Wallet is a Wonderful Thing

by Strenton Mapplwell, 1865

Oh a Yorkshireman's wallet is a wonderful thing
As impregnable as a fort
You can keep stuff in it like your wedding ring
And nobody will get it out.*

Oh a Yorkshireman's wallet is a wonderful thing
Your money is safe in there
Safer than any kind of bank**
You can keep it in a wallet without a care.

Oh a Yorkshireman's wallet is a wonderful thing
It will never reveal its secrets
The inside is a complete enigma***
Like the inside of the earth's core.****

*Note to reader: could you pronounce 'out' as 'ort' to fit with intricate rhyme scheme? Many thanks, SM.
**Note to reader: could you pronounce 'bank' as 'bing' to fit in with the intricate rhyme scheme? Many thanks, SM.
***Note to reader: could you pronounce 'enigma' as 'ening' to fit in with the intricate rhyme scheme? Many thanks, SM.
****Note to reader: could you pronounce 'core' as 'cecrets' to fit in with the intricate rhyme scheme? Many thanks, SM.

FREEZEM

The Yorkshireman's Wallet Pattern Poem

(to be sung)

The Yorkshireman's Wallet
The Wallet
He man's Wallet
The man's Wallet
Yo man Wallet
The man's Wallet
The man Wall
He man Wall
hire Wallet?
The man's Wallet!
The man's Wallet!

AAAtIshoo

BERT'S CHIPPIE

The Invention of the Yorkshireman's Wallet

It was the year 4567BC. Ug, the caveman from Pateley Bridge, had found a berry of the Grodfaglo Tree, one of the rarest of all the trees of the Late Stone Age. It was reputed to have magic healing powers, and he wanted to keep it somewhere safe, away from the marauding hands of his cave-neighbour Ugg.

He sat on a stone, took a stone and began to bash with a stone on the edge of the stone. That was the trouble with the Stone Age: it was monotonous in the extreme. After several months of failed attempts during which he shattered a number of stones, he managed to create a sort of jar or receptacle from stone.

He placed the Grodfaglo berry in the stone jar and it nestled inside, comfortably. He liked the feeling of power over Ugg. He liked the fact that he would never be able to get into the jar to get the berry. He didn't like the fact that he couldn't get into the jar himself. This was not only the first ever known example of The Yorkshireman's Wallet, but also the first known example of a design fault.

Ug took a stone and bashed himself on the head with it, repeatedly.

From the Yorkshireman's Wallet Phrasebook (for use Abroad)

Hello. I am a Yorkshireman and I seem to have mislaid my wallet.

Can you help me please? I am a Yorkshireman and I can't find my wallet.

My wallet has gone/ disappeared/faded away.

My wallet is big/vast/huge/ massive.

My wallet is full/bulging/ straining uncomfortably at the seams.

My wallet has been stolen!

My wallet has been stolen by a thief/robber/cutpurse/ footpad/wallet-mugger!

Can you help me to open my wallet?

I find that I cannot open my wallet.

I need to pay for a drink /meal/tram ticket and I cannot open my wallet, can you help me?

Do you have any pliers/ scissors/a blowtorch/a nuclear device with which I can open my wallet?

I do not tip. I am a Yorkshireman.

YORKSHIRE 722
LANCASHIRE 1

The Yorkshireman's Wallet Alphabet

A is for appy when me wallet is full!
B is for Barry's: it's shaped like a skull.
C is for coins that make my wallet heavy.
D is for Derek's: it looks like Don Revie!
E is for everything I keep in there.
F is for Frank's: it's as big as a chair.
G is for gold: I've got some in this bit.
H is for Harold's what got lost in the flit.
I is for the inside that's never been seen.
J is for Jack's with its own TV screen.
K is for Knaresborough where Kevin bought his.
L is for Larry's: it's an endless abyss.
M is for money, the fine wallet-filler.
N is for Norman's: a suede/leather thriller.
O is what you shout when the wallet you spy!
P is for Peter's: press here, it can fly!
Q is for quality, hand-tooled, hand-made.

R is for Robert's, with badges displayed.
S is for size: X, XL, XXL.
T is for Trevor's: the curve and the swell.
U is umbrella built in the design.
V is for Vic's: it used to be mine.
W is for wallet, the king of the words!
X is for Xavier's: it's Spanish, I've heard.
Y is for yallct. They never caught on.
Z is for Zebedee's: he got it from John.

Wallet Bye-laws from the Village of Dawbury

1. Wallets must not be dropped on the pavement as they will cause a potential trip hazard for pedestrians who will have to use ropes and crampons to climb over them.
2. Wallets must not be left on the dashboards of cars as the driver of the car, as well as all the cars behind it, will not be able to see.
3. Wallets can be no bigger than a mile in length.
4. Wallets must be registered with the Dawbury Wallet Committee and the registration must include the size, weight and provenance of the wallet.
5. Wallets made from the hide of Lancashire cows will not be allowed in the village.
6. Wallets must not be used as overnight shelters unless the shelter is taken in the official campsite near the stream.
7. Wallets must not be used as offensive weapons.

Signed
Walter Moxon, Clerk to the Council.

Now Albert crushes a couple of garlic cloves

Retirement Speech of Enid Naseby

Designer of the 'Nivveroppen Impregnable Yorkshireman's Wallet', first manufactured in 1952.

Friends and colleagues, I should like to take this opportunity to thank you all for coming along today. I have enjoyed forty-three years' continuous service with the company, and I take no little pride in the fact that the fortunes of the firm and of everyone who works and has worked for it have been buoyant because of my invention, the Nivveroppen. As you know, this is a wallet which, once money is placed therein, can, to use the vernacular or the demotic, nivver be oppened.

This is, of course, the Yorkshireman's dream; to have money in his possession that he cannot spend is the apex of his ambitions. As you know, many of our competitors have tried and failed to match the Nivveroppen and indeed a number of them have gone out of business; if I may be allowed to make a small joke here, their versions of the Nivveroppen simply, well, oppened.

(Pause for laughter)

Now, ladies and gentlemen, colleagues, friends; I have

one final task to perform before my retirement. As you know, the secret of the Nivveroppen staying closed was due to my design, which has always been a closely guarded secret, even from you. You'll recall the production line being blindfolded and the senior management walking around with bags over their heads so that they did not learn the secret. Well, today, my last day in this building, you will …

Could you … er … could I have a glass of water …

The secret of … the secret of the … is …

I don't feel very well …

(VOICE OFF: SHE'S COLLAPSED!)

The Best of Class Three's Yorkshireman's Wallet Sentences

I call my door Yorkshireman's Wallet because it doesn't open.

I call my cat Yorkshireman's Wallet because she is very heavy to pick up.

I call storm clouds Yorkshireman's wallets because they are full.

I call my uncle Norman yorkshireman's wallet because he never gives me any money.

I call a broken cup in a box a Yorkshireman's wallet because it jingles when you shake it.

I call the Bank of England a Yorkshireman's Wallet because it is full of money.

I call the Great Wall of China a Yorkshireman's Wallet because it can be seen from space as well.

Uncle Charlie's Wallet

Was tight-lipped, like him.
Had money hidden away, like him.
Worked hard, like him.
Didn't enjoy too much sunlight, like him.

Had a mysterious interior life, like him.
Was once lost on a trip to Weymouth, like him.
Gave nothing away, like him.
Was heavier than it looked, like him.

They buried them side by side.
Auntie Mabel and the bank manager cried.

RIP
BERT
SHUTTLETHORP

FRANS SHUFFLETHORP
THE LAUGHING
YORKSHIREMAN

Yorkshireman's Wallet Fitness DVD

(Music begins …)
Come on everybody!
Come on!
Pick up the wallet, come on, pick it up
Pick it up
Pick it up
I know it's heavy!
Pick it up!
(music swells and becomes rhythmic)
And …
Wait for it …
Lift the wallet
Lift the wallet
Lower the wallet
Lower the wallet
And lift it and … hold …
Hold … hold …
Yes, it's meant to hurt …
Hold … hold …
(music becomes ecstatic)
And lift the wallet
Lift the wallet
Lift the wallet …

The New Yorkshireman's Wallet Corset

From 'Tight-un and Titan Lingerie' of Methley

Ladies and gentlemen: do you feel somewhat …

… *unsupported?*

Do you feel that you are in danger of …

… *spilling all over the place?*

Then you need the new

YORKSHIREMAN'S WALLET CORSET

Yes, THE YORKSHIREMAN'S WALLET

Once fitted by our expert fitter Reginald it is ALMOST IMPOSSIBLE TO REMOVE and will hold your flesh LIKE A GLOVE!

'My figure has never felt fuller and even my feller has noticed thanks to the Yorkshireman's Wallet!' *Mrs B of Kippax.*

'The lads at the mill used to call me "Barrage Balloon" but not any more thanks to the Yorkshireman's Wallet!' *Mr B of Kippax.*

For more details ring Reginald on Methley 854

Overheard Phone Conversation on the 18.50 Train from Barnsley to Leeds

'Aye, she got me a new un. Supposed to be for my birthday. She sez "I've got you this. Your old un's wore art. It's practically dropping to bits." And then she sez "I've chucked it in t' bin anyway. It were no good. Thaz had that wallet years".

'Well, of course, I dashed art but bin men 'ad just been and Ah must've looked a reyt claartead runnin after t' wagon.

'So Ah guz bak int 'ouse and she gid me t' new un.

'An' duz tha know what? It were from Cheshire! It were a Cheshireman's Wallet!

'Hello? Hello? Ah've lost yer ...'

YORKSHIRE

Tell us a Story Uncle Norman

Tell us a story Uncle Norman,
Tell us a story, do
About the time you and Big Jack
Lifted the wallet
In 1962!

It was heavy Uncle Norman,
It weighed a flippin' ton
And you and big Jack heaved and pulled
Till Big Jack's back went
Off like a starting gun!

You decided Uncle Norman
To lift it on your own
The veins on your neck stuck right out
The move did nothing
For your heart or gout!

HOUDINI HOODWINKED!

GREAT ESCAPOLOGIST TRAPPED IN YORKSHIREMAN'S WALLET FOR SEVEN HOURS

'I COULD NOT ESCAPE NO MATTER HOW I TRIED,' SAYS HOUDINI

ESCAPOLOGIST TAKEN TO HOSPITAL WITH MOTH BITES

The great escapologist Harry Houdini remains in hospital after being trapped inside a Yorkshireman's Wallet for

(THE HULL DAILY MAIL 19th February, 1898)

Jerome B Smallett's Yorkshire Wallet

A man called Jerome B Smallett
Was in possession of a very large wallet
He was rich enough to fill it
This extra-large Yorkshireman's Wallet
He chucked Champagne down his gullet
And never emptied his wallet
And never did he spill it
All over his pristine wallet
Then he feasted on red mullet
Bought with riches from his wallet
And a spit-roasted young pullet
Half as big as his king-sized wallet!

Extract from King Lear Act One, The Lost Yorkshireman's Wallet Scene

by William Shakespeare

Fool: Thy lips seem exceeding closed my lord upon thy regal face!

Lear: Mmmm. MmM. MmmM.

Fool: What's that you say? They are as closed as a Yorkshireman's Wallet?

Lear: MmmmMm. MmmmM.

Fool: As you say my liege the Yorkshireman's Wallet is the tightest thing. It is tighter than a thing which is not so tight as that tightness that is the tightness of the thing thereof.

Lear: MmmMMMm.

Fool: Yes, my royal master, you are right. That is an exceeding droll and ticklish joke.

Lear: MmmMMMMM m.

The New Grandma's Corset Wallet

From 'Tight-un and Titan Lingerie' of Methley

Ladies and gentlemen: somebody had a dream.
And the dream came true! Let me tell you a story …

Walking through the lingerie factory one evening
Before the sweepers-up had swept up
Young Tobias Titan, the heir to the Titan fortune,
Noticed piles of lingerie-detritus
Scattered across the floor.
He tripped over some gusset-remains and corset wire
And thought:
'I could turn these shards into something productive!'
And the 'Grandma's Corset Wallet' concept was born.

Now, for a limited time,
You too can own a
GRANDMA'S CORSET WALLET
Made from the kind of material, metal,
wood and whalebone
Your Grandma would have worn.
And it'll never ever open: ask Grandma!

For more details ring Reginald on Methley 854

The Yorkshireman's Wallet and the Bride's Mother

Local radio recently reported the case of Brian Fothergill, of Harrogate, a Yorkshireman who was so in love with his wallet that he insisted on having it in all the photographs of his wedding to his childhood sweetheart Stephanie. Here's a selection of the captions from his album:

Me and Stephanie and the wallet.

Me and Stephanie, informally in the hotel garden with the wallet.

Me and Stephanie and her parents with the wallet.

Me and the wallet.

The wallet on its own.

Stephanie's mother and father and wallet.

Stephanie's mother throwing the wallet away.

Me trying to retrieve the wallet.

Stephanie's mother grabbing the wallet and throwing it into the stream that gurgles by the hotel.

Me jumping in to save it.

Me sitting by the side of the stream having failed to save it.

Stephanie's mother and father in a very happy mood.

THE YORKSHIRE LEANING TOWER OF WALLETS

Bouncy Castle Patent applied for

Mr Trevor Wainwright, of Gronton Terrace, has applied for a patent for a bouncy Yorkshireman's Wallet. Mr Wainwright states that the 'Bouncy Tyke Wallet' will be like a normal bouncy castle in every respect except that it will have zips and a place to keep stamps. He envisages the 'Bouncy Tyke Wallet' will be very popular with sporting groups and stag parties and people who wish they had enough money to fill a wallet of that size. The committee expressed an interest in having a go on the wallet before granting the patent, and, having bounced on it for three and a half hours, declared it to be the greatest invention known to Man and could they all have a free one?

Yorkshireman's Wallet to be Buried in Time Capsule

Today, on the village green at Whatton-super-Cumberworth near Beverley, the citizens of this haven of peace and quiet are gathering to bury a Yorkshire Time Capsule beneath the thousand-year-old Whatton Oak. Items in the capsule include a flat cap, a model of a whippet, a freeze-dried and laminated Yorkshire pudding, a Yorkshire phrase book and a Yorkshireman's Wallet, unopened since the mid-1970s.

Let's move a little closer; shh … I think the ceremony is about to begin. The mayor is about to speak:

THE MAYOR: Ladies and gentlemen and honoured guests, it's our joy today to witness the burying of this Yorkshire Time Capsule which, when it's dug up in a hundred years' time, will reveal to the people of the future the kinds of lives that are led by the people of this corner of Yorkshire …

VOICE OFF: Giz me wallet!

THE MAYOR: … and, er, in the future these as yet unborn people will …

VOICE: You've got me wallet! You're about to bury me wallet!

THE MAYOR: My dear sir, you are interrupting a moment of vital historical importance. I'll call the police!

VOICE: That wallet belongs to me! One of your flunkeys snatched it out of me hand when I was just about to pay for me snap in the pub! Said he needed it for summat!

THE MAYOR: I don't believe you!

FLUNKEY: It's true, sir. I lost the wallet – we were going to bury this gentleman's because after all one Yorkshireman's Wallet is very much like another. Solid. Impenetrable. Full.

THE MAYOR: Good point. Start digging!

YORKSHIRE
SAS
TRAINING
COURSE

Lost Wallet Text Messages

Lst wlt!
    Whr?
If knw tht wdnt b lst!
    Haha. Owt in it?
Full
    R much?
Dunno. Not opnd since 1963.
    U wot?
Not since 1963.
    Yer fool!
Eh?
    Be full on owd money!
Eh?
    Pre decimal! Yer dft haporth.
O. R.

Letter to Father Christmas

Dear Father Christmas

I would like a wallet like my daddy's for Christmas. It is as big as a house. It has a special place to live on a shelf in the front room. If he goes out of the room my daddy tells me to keep an eye on it in case any of the money leaks out. When I ask why it is so big my mam says it is because he has never opened it and put his hand inside and my daddy says that's not true because he opened it in 1983 and my mam doesn't laugh.

I would like a wallet like my daddy's for Christmas because then I would be a real Yorkshireman.

I would also like a wheelbarrow to wheel it around in like my daddy does if that's okay with you.

Love Stephen.

Seven Fateful Minutes for Chaz the Lancashire Pickpocket

Chaz the Lancashire Pickpocket enters Yorkshire to do nefarious things.

Very quickly Chaz spots Derek Fountain making his way from the bank with a wallet full of dosh.

Chaz steals up beside Derek as he ambles down a crowded street.

Chaz seizes his chance and lifts the wallet from the inside of Derek's jacket.

Chaz collapses in pain, holding his wrist, because the wallet is so heavy.

Chaz, pinned beneath the wallet, finds that he cannot move because the wallet is so heavy.

Derek makes a fortune charging visitors (but not Yorkshiremen, of course) to gaze at the trapped Lancashireman.

Walter the Yorkshire Wallet

A book for very small Yorkshire children

Look. Who is this?
This is Walter.
This is Walter the Yorkshire Wallet.
Hello Walter.
Walter, why do you look sad?
Because you are huge and bulgy?
That should make you happy, Walter.
Being huge and bulgy is a good thing
For a wallet, Walter.
Don't cry, Walter.
Go out for a walk. Let people see
How big and bulgy you are.
Repeat after me, Walter:
I AM BIG AND BULGY AND I AM A YORKSHIRE WALLET.
Come on, don't be shy …
I AM BIG AND BULGY AND I AM A YORKSHIRE WALLET.
There, that's better.
Remember, children:
A Yorkshire wallet must ALWAYS be big and bulgy!
ALWAYS!

Yorkshire Dumpty

Yorkshire Dumpty sat on a wallet
Yorkshire Dumpty had a great fall. It
Was miles to the floor cos the wallet was big
So he crushed a bloke who was dancing a jig
At the foot of the wallet. The wallet was vast;
So wide you could have fitted on all of the cast
Of Ben Hur twice then once more again
So no wonder King's horses and all the King's men
Couldn't put Yorkshire Dumpty together again.

A Yorkshireman and a Scotsman meet in a Chip Shop Queue

YORK: Heyop.
SCOT: Och aye.
YORK: Cold out.
SCOT: Aye. Hey, whit's that?
YORK: Me wallet.
SCOT: Ye call that a wallet? That's no a wallet. This is a wallet.

Flourishes wallet

YORK: Well, that is rather large but that was only my toy wallet. This is me real wallet.

Flourishes wallet

SCOT: I've seen bigger Soor Plooms* than that. This, this is what you call a wallet.

Flourishes another wallet with two hands. Begins to sweat from the effort of holding the wallet but refuses to back down.

YORK: Ah, I thought we were talking about wallets. If you want to see a wallet …

Whistles his mate to back his van up to the chip shop door. His mate and some passers-by begin to lever a giant wallet from the back of the van.

SCOT: Ah, if ye want to see a wallet …

Whistles to his mate to lower an enormous wallet towards the chip shop from a crane.

CHIP SHOP OWNER: I wouldn't mind but it's the same every night.

*a Scottish boiled sweet.

CLASSIFIED ADS

WALLETS OPENED WHILE YOU WAIT! Are you a Yorkshireman who simply cannot bear to open his wallet? Has your wallet been sitting on a shelf for years because you can't open it? Do you secretly want to know how much is in your wallet but still can't bring yourself to open it? WE HAVE THE ANSWER! Our Trained Wallet-openers will expertly open your wallet in seconds! If you want them to, they can re-close it again and tell you how much is in there, or not if you don't want them to. Any escaping moths will be released into the wild or hand-reared in our Luxury Wallet Moth Farm. NEVER FEAR: THE WALLET OPENERS ARE HERE! Call Cleckheaton 435.

The Fancy Dress Party

'So Dennis decided to go to the fancy dress party as a Yorkshireman's Wallet; he got me to make him the costume out of an old leather jacket and some scrap metal and I have to admit he looked great.

'He made me make sure that he couldn't open the top of the wallet because he said that made it more authentic. He got to the party and everybody thought the costume was a hit.

'Then, when they were serving refreshments, a waiter accidentally spilled some coffee down the zip and into the costume via the breathing holes. Dennis was trapped because the coffee grounds blocked up the breathing holes and not only was he unable to breathe, he was overheating.

'Still, it'll be something to talk about when he gets out of hospital.'

PUDDING
MIX

THE
PUDDING'S

ZZZ

THE HAUNTING

There. Do you see it? Just there, by the window. Glowing. Somehow suspended in mid-air. The Phantom Wallet. They do say the owner died many years ago without ever opening it and now the wallet is doomed to float in a kind of limbo until someone actually manages to capture it and open it and then somehow it will be released.

That's why I've brought my net. I'll try and catch it. I'll just stretch my arm, get the net higher. Higher … that's it …

Ah! It's zoomed away. I've got a pound coin here. Maybe that'll attract it … Here! Come here … look at this pound … see it glint.

It's getting closer. My goodness, it's beautiful, look at the faux-leather shining in the moonlight. Come on, come on …

Ah! Missed it!

Never mind, better luck next time.

WALLET SHOPPING LIST

Wallet guard.

~~Wallet protector~~.

Wallet opener disabler.

Wallet-carrying trolley.

~~Wallet hoist.~~

~~Wallet straps.~~

Wallet rucksack.

Anti-theft camouflage wallet paint.

~~Anti theft wallet whistle.~~

Book of wallet-carrying exercises.

Wallet wallet.

Wallet wallet cover.

Wallet wallet cover cover.

EE BY
GUMBAY

PUNCH + JUDY

Yorkshireman's Love Poem

I love you more than I love my wallet
And that's saying summat.
My wallet is a beautifully heavy object.
And you are too.
Beautiful I mean, not heavy.
You are not heavy.
But my wallet is heavy.
You are not an object either.
My wallet is an object.

I love you more than I love my wallet
But it's a close-run thing.
My wallet is close to my heart
But not as close as you.
Although literally it is
Because it is in my inside pocket
For protection.
And you would not fit
In my inside pocket.
I think I'd better
Stop this poem now
And write a different one.

BARNSLEY

The Yorkshireman's Wallet Galaxy

At the far end of the universe
There is an object
A heavy object spinning through space
A vast galaxy shaped like a Yorkshireman's Wallet
And it's heavy
Really heavy
Hence the name ...

And it's moving
And getting closer
And closer

And the stars are rattling like change
And the cosmic gas is like a ten pound note
And the asteroids are like house keys

And it's getting closer
And closer
And closer ...